F391.2.H638L6

1350575

SOUTH CAMPUS LIBRARY
TARRANT COUNTY
JUNIOR COLLEGE
FT. WORTH, TEXAS 76119

# WILL HOGG, *Texan*

WILL HOGG

# WILL HOGG, *TEXAN*

*By* JOHN A. LOMAX

AUSTIN : 1956
UNIVERSITY OF TEXAS PRESS
*Published for the* HOGG FOUNDATION

Copyright 1940 by *The Atlantic Monthly*
*Reprinted by permission*

# Foreword

Vigor, fearlessness, downright honesty, and a love for the state of Texas and its people marked all the years of Will Hogg's life. These traits remain alive today in the bequests Will Hogg left to the University of Texas for the use of the people of the state.

John A. Lomax, folklorist, in the article *Will Hogg, Texan,* captured and portrayed this rare combination of characteristics that made Will Hogg a leader in his day and a tradition in the state for all time. The Hogg Foundation is pleased to make this account of its founder available to a large reading audience by republishing the *Atlantic Monthly* article in book form.

Any history of Texas would be incomplete without mention of Governor James Stephen Hogg and the entire Hogg family. In his final bequest, Will Hogg, the Governor's son, left the residue of his estate for the benefit of Texans, natives and newcomers alike. His brother Mike and his sister, Ima, chose to carry on this interest of their brother by establishing in his honor the Hogg Foundation for Mental Hygiene. His brother Tom left his estate to the Hogg Foundation, after the life interest of his widow. Miss Ima Hogg and the widows of both Mike and Tom have made generous financial arrangements with the university for the benefit of the Hogg Foundation.

Will Hogg's strong devotion to Texas made it appropriate for him to establish a unique foundation that would perpetuate his life purposes. The Hogg Foundation for Mental Hygiene, organized in 1940, has endeavored to further his aspirations in three ways.

1. Will Hogg was devoted to the University of Texas; he founded its Ex-Students' Association and fought the university's battles whenever its standards or freedom were endangered. The foundation, as an arm of the university, works with all other departments and branches, calling frequently upon the president of the university for guidance in planning. Other administrative officials and faculty members have also given invaluable assistance to the foundation.

2. Will Hogg was expansive in his ideals and interests. He established loan funds in colleges throughout the entire state and left his money to be used for the benefit of the many. The foundation's statewide program of Mental Health Education, Service and Research has already reached into more than 300 Texas communities of all sizes.

3. Will Hogg carried on his father's interest

in the welfare of the people and the institutions that served them. The foundation has endeavored to continue this ideal, not only through its concern for the mentally ill, but also through its work with citizen and professional groups that aspire to improve human relations and the mental health of all people.

Will Hogg was wise and forthright like his father. John Lomax has given us glimpses of his colorful life and personality. The university and the foundation have assumed a responsibility and are constantly stimulated by the example of their founder in carrying it out.

>ROBERT L. SUTHERLAND
>Director
>The Hogg Foundation for Mental Hygiene

October 10, 1956

# Contents

| | |
|---|---|
| Foreword | vii |
| Two Giant Texans | 3 |
| Egg Money | 8 |
| Watchdog of the University | 14 |
| Gambler on Brains and Ambition | 22 |
| "Blue Books" and Crape Myrtle | 26 |
| Nickels for Neckties | 35 |
| The "Tender Tempest" | 44 |

# Illustrations

Will Hogg *Frontispiece*
    Drawing by Malcolm Thurgood

James Stephen Hogg 5
    Drawing by Malcolm Thurgood

Varner Plantation *Front End Paper*
    Drawing by E. M. Schiwetz

Will Hogg's Home in Houston *Back End Paper*
    Drawing by E. M. Schiwetz

# Two Giant Texans

One day in the early part of this century two men, father and son, sat talking together on the long veranda of the historic Varner Plantation manor house, fifty miles southwest of Houston, Texas. They were strikingly alike in stature and depth of chest, in the tawny coloring of their hair, in their wide firm mouths, their grayish-blue eyes, ruddy complexions, and deep resonant voices. The father was a man mountain, over six feet tall and weighing in his prime nearly three hundred pounds; the son was slightly smaller. Now the tired old lion, ex-Governor

"Jim" Hogg, sensing perhaps the end of his days, had asked his son, Will Hogg, to leave his work in St. Louis and come home to Texas.

"Until that six months I spent talking with my father," said Will Hogg long afterwards, "I had never really known him. I had just taken him for granted. Then for the first time I understood why he had always espoused the cause of the common people, the need of battling for the weak against the strong, the necessity of free education for all, if a democracy is to survive. So I came to love more deeply this plantation, this farmhouse, and my father. Whatever little good I may do, whatever ideals may be found behind any action of mine, whatever has given my life any worth or dignity, all are due to him."

As governor of a pioneer state, James Stephen Hogg, the son of a brigadier general of the Confederacy, fostered many pioneer laws, among them the one ending the free-pass system on Texas railroads; another establishing the first

JAMES STEPHEN HOGG

Railroad Commission for government regulation of railways; still another "squeezing the mud and water" out of railroad stocks and bonds, and forbidding the further issuance of fraudulent public securities. Probably his most important law forbade the ownership of large bodies of Texas land by out-of-the-state corporations. On leaving public office Governor Hogg, like Robert E. Lee, refused handsome retainers from corporations seeking his influence, and he declined also all legal employment that involved the constitutionality, or even the interpretation, of laws regulating corporations that had been passed on his recommendation.

After the father's death the Varner Plantation became a holy place for Will Hogg and his sister, "Missima," and for the two brothers, Mike and Tom. Will once said, "I tried to fix up the old place as George Washington would do if he had a bank roll." The two towering live oaks at the entrance will long stand to remind pilgrims of two giant Texans, father and son—the spot marking for one the close, for the other the beginning, of a notable career. In making Texas a better place to live in, Governor Hogg had the aid of high office. His chief rival, Judge George Clark, of Waco, once said: "He had a power of dominating his followers that I have never seen excelled in any man." His son, fired with the ideals of the father and inheriting his powers of leadership, acquired wealth that gave him independence and freedom to strike hard blows for any righteous cause. His fortune came largely through black gold, Texas oil—much of it from those wide fields upon which father and son looked as they talked and planned together on the veranda at West Columbia.

# Egg Money

Will Hogg made his home in Houston. There he became associated with J. S. Cullinan and James L. Autry, prominent officials of the Texas Company. These three men refused to follow the company when its headquarters were moved to New York City. Instead, they formed a corporation of their own, the Farmers Oil Company, acquired an abandoned oil field, deepened the wells by a thousand feet or so, and struck a new oil stratum which soon poured out riches at a reported rate of sixty dollars for each dollar invested. This one venture made Will Hogg a rich man.

Late in life ex-Governor Hogg himself had become interested in oil through the discovery of the famous Spindletop field at Beaumont, Texas. He found bubbles coming up through the marshy lowlands of the Varner Plantation at West Columbia, fifty miles from Houston—bubbles, some said, which would burst into flames when touched by a lighted match. Here was the possibility of a heritage for his children not provided by his otherwise small estate. He bought the plantation, comprising some 5,000 acres, and his will requested that his children should not sell the land for ten years. Several years after his death, during the period of World War I, one of the big oil companies explored the Varner Plantation and sank a well with an initial flow of 100,000 barrels of oil. Since that time this field has produced an estimated total of a hundred million barrels. When the first big well came in, Will cabled the news to his brother Mike, then on the firing line in France, and asked what should be done with Mike's share of the fortune. Mike cabled: "Ship me a dozen cases of eggs."

With the income from the profitable West Columbia oil field of the Hogg estate, Will Hogg became the senior partner and directing manager of Hogg Brothers, the firm including himself, Mike Hogg, Tom Hogg, and Miss Ima Hogg. At the same time he managed his own properties and served as investment trustee for other estates. Levelheaded Mike, always at his side, acted as a brake to the impulsive and emotional outbursts of the dynamic and dominating elder brother. Among the early investments was an eight-story office building in Houston, the entire top floor of which was reserved for the offices of Hogg Brothers. A strip of sod several feet wide runs around the entire rim of the eighth-floor roof; here Will Hogg planted flowers and a young forest of shrubbery, perennially green in the semitropical climate. The main executive office was a big, high-ceilinged room with two capacious flat-topped desks and armchairs, one for Mike and one for Will—the latter's being a special job, oversize, because he overflowed the ordinary chair just as he overflowed everything else that he touched. Around the walls were hung Remington paintings—"The Herd Boy," "The Fight at the Water Hole," "The Cry for Help"—and nearby a portrait of Governor Hogg. On a projection in one corner of the roof garden Will built a suite of rooms, bedroom, oval dining room, and kitchen, where he often entertained parties of friends and business callers. Once when a friend told Will that the gossips whispered that these rooms were used as a bagnio, he replied without rancor: "I don't care what they think or say as long as Mike and Raymond Dickson will visit my grave once in a while."

From Hogg Brothers stemmed various subsidiary corporations, the chief one, perhaps, being the Varner Realty Company, which invested mainly in Houston property and oil lands.

Among the successful real estate ventures of this company was the promotion of 2,000 lots for persons of limited income. Every lot was sold and paid for under the generous terms provided. At one time the company, in partnership with Raymond Dickson, owned a large cotton warehousing and exporting business. For several years Will Hogg interested himself in the Wilson process for making women's shoes and spent a lot of money securing patents. This attempt to buck the shoe machinery monopoly, like other ventures, as he once said, "mildewed and turned green on us in the summertime." He financed and promoted the Findex system of filing and sold his interests at a profit. In partnership with one of his lawyers, David Picton, he furnished funds for making Ingleside, on Corpus Christi Bay, a deep-water port from which oil tankers daily take cargoes for the four corners of the earth. He took options on extensive coal properties in Kentucky and Tennessee and other options on gold mines in Mexico. He cherished an unfulfilled ambition to own a producing gold mine. One of the unvalued items of his final gift to the University of Texas was a batch of Cripple Creek, Colorado, gold-mining stock.

"Will Hogg was no businessman," contemptuously remarked the president of one of Houston's big oil companies. "All his money came through the friendship of J. S. Cullinan and from his father's land at West Columbia." Will's spacious office, to be sure, was not a place where shrewd, undercover, overreaching trades were executed. Rather it became a mecca to which traveled those who needed help, where worthy causes were aided, where were born many movements for the common good. Here was a healthy mixture of sound business judgment and high-minded business ideals, carried out by an efficient organization under the leadership of a resourceful personality.

# Watchdog of the University

Will Hogg was still in his thirties when he attained financial independence. Although he was at the head of an organization managing the business and investments of several large estates, "I did this with my left hind foot," he said afterwards; "there was bigger game abroad." As the Houston *Gargoyle* remarked, he became a sort of "Superintendent of Everybody's Business." First and foremost was his interest in public education in Texas. He had grown tired of seeing its university kicked around. While he was yet a salaried employee of the Texas Company, he adopted a unique plan for raising Texas from the low educational brackets. He made his first "Blue Book," which called for the expenditure within five years of not less than a quarter of a million dollars "to stimulate thought and create and arouse, through bulletins and lectures, aspiration for higher education in Texas." The signers of the "Blue Book" were to be "good citizens of Texas who necessarily are and must be deeply concerned in the individual culture of themselves and their posterity." At the beginning he was asked what he would do if donors could not be found. "I'm worth a total of thirty thousand dollars," he replied. "That's enough to run the shebang for a year. I'll dump that into the pot and let the doubters see the results." He traveled at his own expense throughout Texas and secured subscriptions from wealthy men for more than the designated sum. Ultimately the special constitutional tax for higher education at which he aimed was killed by rivalry over the division of its income, if and when voted. The experiment failed. Nonetheless, interest in higher education was aroused, and Will Hogg became known as its ardent champion. This championship was needed when James E. Ferguson was elected governor.

Governor Jim, the husband of Governor "Ma" Ferguson—for whom later, through two terms, he "carried in the wood and toted the water"—had little use for higher education. After he assumed office, Governor Ferguson declared that "too many people are going hog-wild over higher education." He, or his friends, disliked eight men on the faculty of the University of Texas, and he demanded that these professors be "fired," on the charge that they were engaged in an "unholy spree of establishing an educational hierarchy." Of Professor William J. Battle, acting president and for twenty-eight years professor of Greek, he said to the Board of Regents, with Will Hogg presiding as chairman: "You keep that man Battle here and you lay a precedent that tells every Governor for forty years that they have no right to do as they want to." Will Hogg met this declaration of unbridled autocracy with the retort: "I for one would rather go to hell in a handbasket than to act without investigation of charges."

Later, after Mr. Hogg's term as regent had expired, a supine Board of Regents did discharge without any hearing six members of the university faculty. Soon thereafter the Governor vetoed the entire appropriation of $1,600,000 for the University of Texas which the Legislature had granted for two years. The university lay stricken and helpless until Will Hogg came to Austin, where, leasing a half-floor of the Driskill Hotel, he spent a long hot summer. He and Chester H. Terrell, his able classmate of San Antonio, declared ruthless war on "Farmer Jim." No Governor could "put the putrid paw of politics on the University of Texas."

One impeachment charge against Governor Ferguson was followed by another. Texans had probably not been so deeply aroused since the Civil War as they were by the dramatic incidents that followed. The friends of the Governor came to Austin in crowds, among them a detachment of Texas Rangers, pistols on hips, wearing ten-gallon hats. Governor Ferguson kept one of the noted gunmen always at his side. At night two others sat in rocking chairs on the front porch of the Governor's Mansion. Former students and friends of the university rallied in support of Will Hogg and his cause. During the excitement friends urged him to arm himself against assassination. "Hell, they won't shoot." And he went on unobtrusively about his job.

He said in an interview: "How far this cheerful and constructive autocrat will be able to travel the rocky road of his mad career is measured entirely by the forbearance and apathy of the best citizenship of the state and by the trifling percentage of illiteracy and ignorance to which alone he can appeal with any assurance of temporary success. . . . My prediction is that he is riding to the biggest fall, personally and politically, in the short and simple annals of the misguided politicians of Texas." Again, dedicating a volume containing a stenographic report of the first impeachment investigation (the publication of which he paid for out of his own pocket), he wrote: "To the people of Texas whose Governor has disgraced and degraded our University by securing a Board of Regents a majority of whom servilely do his will; by falsely accusing members of the Faculty and having them dismissed, notwithstanding their acquittal . . . and when called to answer for his misdeeds announces: 'I don't have to give reasons; I am Governor' . . . to the people in their hour of humiliation, this record is dedicated."

"When the law gets in the way of practical business it don't mean anything," announced the Governor. The Senate thought differently when the Governor refused to disclose the source of $156,000 paid in cash to him in his office. They voted twenty-seven to four for his removal from office.

Following the Ferguson upheaval, letters and telegrams and personal appeals urged Will Hogg to permit his name to be proposed for governor. "You won't have to run," they begged; "your name is enough." He replied: "I'm not running for office and I never will. I won't wear a ball and chain on my leg while I am fighting those coyotes who are befouling the name of the State of Texas. I'd rather be a rock-throwing private soldier with a free voice than be the mouthpiece of an organization that would tell me when to talk and what to say."

There were other times that the University of Texas watchdog showed his teeth. Will Hogg once learned that the Board of Regents had sold in secret, without competitive bids, contrary to all legal precedents, a three-million-dollar issue of bonds against the credit of the university. From New York City, Will notified four members of the board by wire that the trade must be canceled or else. . . . It was canceled in great privacy, though it took these harried officials nearly a year to shake off the brokers who had bought the securities.

# Gambler on Brains and Ambition

"In a well-ordered democracy," Will Hogg once declared, "no boy or girl with brains and character should be denied the opportunity of college training. I find that nothing else gives me half the satisfaction derived from the knowledge that I have gambled on the brains and ambition of young men and young women. If I knew just when I was going to die, beyond my funeral expenses I wouldn't reserve enough money to buy a bowl of chili." At the close of World War I he authorized a university official, after pledging him not to reveal the donor, to advertise in all Texas papers that any ex-soldier who could enter the university would be provided with necessary funds. Letters came from five hundred, and more than a hundred ex-soldiers actually enrolled. He sponsored a movement that resulted in subscriptions for $300,000 to aid worthy students wishing to attend the University of Texas. For students of exceptional promise who wished to do graduate or professional work outside of Texas he privately provided funds. In most of these cases he so covered his tracks that his benefactions cannot be traced.

In 1925 a friend told him that Tom Douglas Spies wished to go to the Harvard Medical School. To him, through the university's Ex-Students Association, for four years went Will Hogg's checks to cover expenses. He never saw young Spies. In fact, he did not wish the young man to know the real source of the money. Only

24 •

Will Hogg's death brought disclosure. In the *Annals of Internal Medicine* of March, 1939, a committee of the American College of Physicians announced: "The Committee on Fellowships and Awards recommends that the John Phillips Memorial Medal for 1939 be awarded to Dr. Tom Douglas Spies for outstanding contributions to the science of nutrition, and particularly for his studies in the nature and character of pellagra."

In all such loans—and there were many—it was understood that the money repaid by the young graduates should go back to the University of Texas to be available for other young scientists. During his lifetime Will Hogg provided a model charter for a student loan fund and made an initial cash gift to fourteen Texas colleges. From his estate $450,000 has been put into Rice Institute in Houston, and into thirteen state tax-supported institutions of higher learning, including $25,000 to the Negro college at Prairie

View—these funds to aid worthy boys and girls seeking college training. The residue of his property was transferred to the University of Texas. To that institution he gave much of his life; dying, he gave it nearly all his remaining accumulated wealth, estimated to exceed two million dollars. Another million he gave to education during his lifetime, two million to allied social benefits. By his persuasive eloquence he raised two and a half million more. Thus, through his hands for the common good has come seven million dollars. This much is known. Not even his family can tell what he gave away privately.

# "Blue Books" and Crape Myrtle

In his devotion to the state and its university, Will Hogg did not fail to see the needs of his home city, Houston. Oil, lumber, and a deep-water port poured wealth into this growing industrial center. Millionaires sprouted overnight from oil fields that surround the city closely and spread for hundreds of miles around. "Through the leavening influence of beauty in our city," he once told a group of friends, "I want to help save ourselves from the crass commercialism that comes along with quickly accumulated wealth." He organized a Forum of Civics with these words from Pericles as its motto: "No Athenian should ever confess that he neglected public service for the sake of private fortune." The forum he described as

an organization designed to stimulate civic pride and to combine many and varied forces for the betterment of our city and county. For the improvement of the community in its physical, social, educational or economic aspects . . . the enduring existence of which depends solely upon the spirit existing in the minds and hearts of the members of the Forum. . . . Underlying the stated purposes of such an organization there must be the basic desire to make this city more enjoyable, more adequately equipped, more beautiful—and consequently more useful for everyone who lives and works therein. . . . As the budget of this organization is underwritten, the payment of dues or other pecuniary contributions are to be truly voluntary, unsolicited and unexpected.

At a cost of $50,000 or more, he and the Hogg estate financed the forum, including 10,000 copies of the beautiful *Garden Book,* illustrated in color, costing $10,000, and distributed free. From the Forum of Civics came the report of the City Planning Commission, W. C. Hogg, chairman, the results of which are helping to make Houston a beautiful city. In closing this report Will Hogg wrote:

When we build let us build forever. Let it not be for the present delight or for the present use alone. Let it be such work that our descendants will thank us for, and let us think, as we lay stone on stone, that a time is to come that these stones will be held sacred because our hands have touched them and that men will say, as they look upon our labor and the wrought substance of them, "See! This our fathers did for us."

In a signed public letter charging a popular mayor with attempting to divert to his own ends the plans of the commission, he denounced him "for his suave sophistry, ruinous procrastination and infidelity to the city.... Even if he were honest in every particular and hadn't recently lied. ... I would be against him for many reasons."

He gave eleven reasons for opposing the official's re-election; the last one reads: "In all my contacts with him I have never detected the slightest emotion for, or any real affectionate interest in, the finer things of city building or city service."

Throughout years of planning and discussion he was buying privately and securing options on hundreds of acres of desirable sections for city parks, his agents working quietly so as to prevent unreasonable prices. When at last the city was ready to go into the market for land, Will Hogg handed over the 1,200 acres for Memorial Park at precisely the price he had contracted for, although in the meantime real estate values had increased 500 per cent. In addition, he gave to the city $50,000 to enable it to buy a needed tract. Two other Houston parks, Herman and McGregor, owe much of their present-day beauty and completion to the insistence of Will Hogg. For a considerable period he was the anonymous donor of $30,000 a year with which to purchase crape-myrtle plants for the city parks and private homes. With each package of plants went two tags, one a pledge of the citizen to plant the shrubs on his ground, the second carrying explicit directions for planting and caring for the shrubs for two years. Will Hogg learned that the "white folks" were getting all the shrubs. Thereupon he bought thousands more which were given out only at Emancipation Park, the Negroes' recreation center, to brighten the dooryards of Houston's Negro district. The 1,500-acre residential section of River Oaks, on which he expended three million dollars and out of which during his lifetime he is said to have made no profit, is one of the show places of Houston. In River Oaks, on Lazy Lane, he made his home with his sister, Miss Ima, among pine and oak trees that he had nurtured.

Houston's $350,000 Art Museum was largely the result of his intense devotion to the city's welfare. Another of his "Blue Books" listed

$326,000 in pledges secured by him. When asked to lead a movement to raise funds, he would grin and say: "They want me to work on the aesthetic side. I'm glad to. The government made a mistake originally in not reserving for its own use all the wealth below the soil. What I don't pay back in taxes on the oil which should not have been mine, I'm glad to give away for the public welfare." A Houston man declared that many men of the city felt complimented when Will Hogg came along with a "Blue Book" and asked them to chip in with five thousand or so. To an oil millionaire who refused to subscribe he wired: "It's a damn shame that a man of your means, insight, and ability will stint his spiritual and intellectual growth by staying out of such an unselfish enterprise, especially when the amount and terms of payment involved are relatively ridiculous compared to the significance of your sharing in the beauty and joy of this gift to this beloved community, and may God bless you."

A home for newsboys, the Boy Scouts, the Girl Scouts, organized charity—a thousand and one causes were never denied his help. Just before his death he evolved plans for a new million-dollar building for the Houston Young Men's Christian Association. At the same time he was busying himself with a movement to rebuild entirely the city's Negro section.

There was nothing sanctimonious about him. Humor was present in all such work. A committee of Houston ladies, soliciting money for a new building for the Young Women's Christian Association, were shocked to find Will Hogg an unsympathetic listener.

"But why?" they complained. "Everybody has told us that you are very generous."

"Ladies," he answered, "these young girls, strangers coming to the growing city, certainly need the care and protection that your organization throws about them. I find no fault with that. But why stumble along with a paltry hundred thousand dollars? The small sum you ask for is only chicken feed. I'll help you if you strike for half a million, and go after it this way...."

His enthusiasm grew as he talked. The result was that the committee left his office having surrendered the entire plan into his hands. To carry it out cost him his vacation. In a beautifully embossed blue leather-bound book, dedicated to the good women of Houston, blank spaces were left for signatures. Each signature cost its owner $5,000. All that summer Will Hogg plodded about the streets of Houston, "Blue Book" under arm, on what he called a "gumshoe campaign, highjacking my friends." One lady complained that a breakfast in her home cost her $10,000; Will Hogg happened in with his "Blue Book," and before the eggs were finished she and her husband had signed up. Gradually a total sum of $850,000 was subscribed. As always, Will Hogg topped the list in amount given, though his own name was unobtrusively inserted far down the list. Not all the subscriptions came easily. The beloved Episcopal rector, Dr. Peter Gray Sears, declared that Will Hogg "cussed" the Young Women's Christian Association building into existence.

# Nickels and Neckties

There was a human, personal side to Will Hogg that always appealed to me even more deeply than his valiant, and often violent, fights for civic righteousness. His fury against any hampering of the University of Texas grew solely out of the fact that through it he believed the enlightenment of all the people might come. He had little sympathy for that love of alma mater that expends itself in grotesque costumes and noisy hullabaloos. As a student at the University of Texas, he had his own small circle of intimates, and at that time I knew him but slightly, though for a year we lived in the same dormitory. Despite his modesty, to me, raw and green from the country, the glamour surrounding the son of a distinguished Governor created a bar to easy friendship. Afterwards, when he became president of the Ex-Students Association, I was its salaried secretary. So, through years of association, I came to know some of the wise tenderness of the man.

Throughout the time that I was a minor official at the University of Texas, I had from him this standing order: "When any student in the University of Texas gets into trouble, help him. As long as he is on the rolls of the University he is my ward. If he needs money, lend it to him. If he is sick, get a doctor. If he gets thrown into jail, bail him out. If he dies and has no money or people, bury him. Don't wait to write or wire me; relieve the distress and then let me know at what cost." "And," he added with savage grimness, "if you ever let anyone know where the money comes from, I'll — I'll never send you another blankety-blank cent for any featherheaded scheme as long as I live." Recently a prominent Texas lawyer told me: "While I was a student in the University, I once borrowed enough money from you to buy a suit of clothes. I had to back out of your office. You see, I was wearing my last pair of trousers and they were gone in the rear." This gentleman never knew that it was Will Hogg's money that patched his pants.

One day Will Hogg called on a classmate in San Antonio and asked him for a contribution to the Student Loan Fund.

"Mr. Hogg," objected the man, "when I attended the University I paid my own way. I asked for no favors. I graduated, and since that time I have become well established and I have achieved some success through my own efforts. You now come and ask me to give money to that institution. I'd like for you to tell me what the University of Texas has ever done for me."

"Not a blankety-blank thing!" thundered Will Hogg as he gathered up his papers and left the room.

In Fort Worth he once invited a group of University of Texas men to lunch with him. Over the coffee he explained in detail his plans for the University of Texas, pleading for generous gifts. His earnestness failed to arouse any response except for a few small donations. Will Hogg grew angry. He was volunteering his time, paying his own expenses, even buying the lunch for the group. But the Fort Worth people were failing to do their part. Finally his scorn flamed: "You can do precisely as you please. You can give the money or not. But I'll get Fort Worth's share before I leave town. If you boys don't come across, I know where I can get it. I'm going out on the streets and collect the money from the whores and the hack-drivers. They'll help a good cause."

The conductor of the Golden Gate Limited on the run between San Antonio and Houston paused one morning to chat with a group of passengers in the smoking room. Politics was in the air, and soon the talk veered in that direction. Said the conductor, "There's one man I'd like to vote for if he would ever run for office. His name is Will Hogg, old Governor Jim Hogg's son. I never saw him but once, but what happened then was enough to win me."

"Tell us the story," suggested a passenger.

"I was pulling this same train out of San Antonio about a year ago," said the conductor. "There we had taken on a lunger who was traveling back to Alabama with his wife. He was in a bad way. Six months in the land of sunshine had failed to help his tuberculosis. He said he wanted to die in his old home. We put him in his berth. His anxious wife had reason to be uneasy, for the man died on the train before we were fifty miles out of the city.

"When I went to tell his wife that under the rules she would be required to take her husband's body off the train at the next stop, I found a big, deep-voiced man in a brown suit on the seat beside her. He wasn't saying much, only sitting around, handing her water and trying to make himself useful. When I spoke to her she broke down and began to cry. The man in the brown suit followed me into the next coach and stopped me.

" 'Listen,' he said, 'you can't put this woman and her dead husband off the train in a little jerkwater town. It's inhuman and I won't stand for it.'

" 'But it's the law. I have no choice.'

" 'To hell with the law! My name is Will Hogg. I live in Houston. I know the head officials of the Southern Pacific, and I'll take all the responsibility. They won't touch you—I guarantee that. I'll wire ahead and arrange everything.'

"And he did. Most of the time he was back there in the sleeping car talking to that woman and trying to make her comfortable.

"When the long train came to a stop in Houston, waiting at the steps was a lovely woman with her arms full of flowers. They told me it was Miss Ima, Will Hogg's sister. They helped that strange woman off the car, and the last I saw of them Will and Miss Ima both had their arms around her, guiding her into a big automobile pulled up close to the curb."

The conductor paused.

"There's the sort of palooka that gets my vote, from United States Senator on up," he added.

One Christmas morning I visited Will Hogg at the Claridge Hotel in New York. I found him unwrapping packages. The assortment ranged from American Beauty roses to a half-dozen choice Virginia hams.

"Here's a package from home," he said. "Let's see what's in it." He unrolled six or seven silk neckties. Inside were nearly a hundred penciled signatures on a long strip of paper whose margins were splotched with smudgy fingerprints:

Christmas Greetings—To Mr. Will Hogg from his friends, the newsboys of Houston, Texas

Will Hogg held aloft the ties, fingered them, and then walked over to the window and looked down on Broadway far below. He stood with his back to me for a long time. When he turned around, as if angry at his tears he blurted out: "The damned little rascals! They ought to be horsewhipped for spending their nickels on me. I don't need any neckties. Why, by God. . . ." He choked again and turned back to the window.

Fred Scott, for thirty-five years a redcap at the Southern Pacific depot in Houston, shook his head sadly when I asked him about Will Hogg.

"He was the Negroes' friend. We went to him with all our troubles. He would always intercede for us. Once when his cook's little boy stuck a rusty nail in his foot, Mr. Hogg took him to St. Joseph's Hospital and told them to put him in a private room and take good care of him. And they did for a long time. It cost Mr. Will a thousand dollars.

"When the train pulled in, Mr. Will would always holler out, 'Scott!' I'd come a-runnin' and take care of his valises. Every time he gave me a dollar. He was never crabbed with me. Other gentlemen were loose with their money, too, but they never said, 'Much obliged.' Mr. Will was a busy man, but he would stop and smile and say that."

Scott slumped in his seat. "Everything's as dark as an iron safe since Mr. Will's gone. We have no one to turn to. We're just lost."

# The "Tender Tempest"

After days of work—as he once put it, "days when I cook up pills to gag the local inhabitants"—Will Hogg periodically would "light and look at his saddle." He made long visits to Hollywood and New York City. He visited South American resorts with Irvin S. Cobb, who for ten consecutive years hunted from Will's lodge at Aransas Pass. Now and then he made long, leisurely trips through Europe.

When friends were not traveling with him he picked up friends on the way. He played the game of life as lustily and with as much gusto during his vacations as he did when he kept his office force of twenty or thirty men humming while he was at home.

Will Hogg owned no golf sticks. He did not hunt or fish or ride. Fond of camping out, he busied himself on such trips as a kitchen subaltern to see that everyone had enough to eat. Alvin, a Southern Negro cook in New York City, would often be summoned to his Park Avenue apartment to cook "Mr. Will's" favorite chili con carne. Even in Paris, where his beloved chili was unknown, another Negro from the South was set up in business only because of his skill and knowledge in putting together this appetizing dish. But talkative Ike, chef at West Columbia, remained the favorite. "Ike's the best garbage cook in the world," declared Will Hogg. "You can't beat one of his meals of fried catfish, country sausage, young mustard greens, black-eyed peas or Mexican frijoles, buttermilk, with a dash of potlikker for an appetizer."

No one who reads this chronicle would believe that Will Hogg was inherently shy. He was forceful always in office conference, but public speaking filled him with terror. His few public addresses made vernacular history, some of it unprintable. He could be poetically profane, he could cuss by note, often using words that are not or should not be in the dictionary. Vivid, keen, contradictory, fiery, dynamic, rough, he was never malicious. The gruff, brusque outward manner concealed a great, sentimental, generous man within. "A man has to love him a lot to keep from killing him," sighed a suffering business associate one day.

This "tender tempest" either had to cuss things out or break down and weep like a child. (His tears choked him to silence twice as he begged the regents not to elect a politician president of the University of Texas.) Selfishness, injustice, the hypocrisy of scheming politicians, drove him to fury. When George W. Littlefield, a millionaire stockman and banker, led the fight on the University of Texas under directions from Governor Ferguson, Will told him: "Major, I'm going to talk to you like no man ever talked to you before. You've been the bull-tongued banker in a one-horse town, sitting up in your saffron-colored cage so long that you've lost the power to tell right from wrong." Then the fearless Major listened to a lurid description of his ancestry—and he didn't shoot.

Mose was Will's chauffeur. One day Mike Hogg noticed that Mose looked gloomy and down in the mouth.

"What's the matter, Mose?" inquired Mike.

"I'm just feelin' bad," answered Mose. "I ain't havin' no luck. Mr. Will ain't cussed me in a long time. You know, when he cusses me a little, he always gives me a dollar; when he gives me a big cussin', I gits five dollars. But he ain't cussed me no time lately, big *or* little . . . and I needs the money."

Will Hogg bequeathed Mose $1,000 for each of his ten years of service to the family. A similar sum was given to each personal household servant of his home in Houston and of his New York apartment.

His friends sometimes called him "William Combustible Hogg." He was always a man's man. No one who ever knew him doubted just where he stood. Always he fought in the open. It should be added that, though his influence was often solicited, he usually avoided taking any part in political scrambles. But he struck hard. After accusing one of his wealthy fellow-townsmen of shady financial deals, he concluded his signed statement with this phrase: "A consistent and calculating career of mendacity which would belittle even Jesse James, who was romantic enough to ride a horse." There was no reply, no libel suit. No one talked back.

Nor did Will Hogg do things to be seen of men. "I don't like the blankety-blank guff of newspapers." He once threatened Odd McIntyre: "If you put my name in your column of tripe, I'll kick you so hard you'll taste leather the rest of your life."

At the close of a campaign of terrific effort for the Houston Art Museum, he got wind of a public reception to be held in his honor and fled from Houston. Another time a great gathering of citizens planned in secret a reception at the Rice Hotel to present him with a diamond-studded medal "for having rendered the people of Houston the most distinguished service of the year." To throw him off his guard a small group of prominent men, headed by the president of the First National Bank, invited him to a private dinner at the hotel. Becoming suspicious, he feigned illness and left his office early, rode home, and went to bed. Nor would he budge from it.

He played at being a gem-collector and a connoisseur and patron of art, and came to own eighty-five Remingtons. All his jewelry he gave away. In trying to help Maclyn Arbuckle and a group of penniless actors he fruitlessly spent a hundred thousand dollars on a moving-picture experiment in San Antonio. He angeled a Broadway show for Earl Carroll. When trouble came to Carroll he used his powerful influence to secure his release from prison. He seemed never to tire of giving. A companion told me, "One night I saw eleven panhandlers touch him in a single block in Hollywood, and each carried away something." He surrounded himself with "laughter and the love of friends." He found pleasure in giving Christmas presents, though he suffered tortures when thanked for his favors. He enjoyed his playground in Old Mexico, where he and his friend, Raymond Dickson, shared ownership in a ranch stocked with thousands of cattle. Though it was twice the size of Manhattan, with a Spanish castle in its center, he called it "a little patch with a sick cow and a sour well."

Irvin Cobb spoke of Will Hogg as of all men the most lovable, most self-effacing, most generous. Ex-Attorney General Watt Gregory said that he was the most vivid personality Texas will ever know. O. O. McIntyre wrote in his column: "Some day I hope to hear him shout, 'Hello, Splinters! How in hell did you get up here?'"

As for me, I shall always like best to think of him as he stood in his room in New York City, with tear-dimmed eyes, stroking lovingly a handful of silk neckties which the newsboys of Houston had sent him for Christmas.

The resolute man, unbeset by fear, acts promptly and decisively. Thus he fights public wrong as effectively when alone as if he led an army with banners. When his fight is ended he leaves behind a precious and everlasting heritage: the timid take heart and renew their courage in the memory of an heroic soul.—
*The Modern Marcus Aurelius*

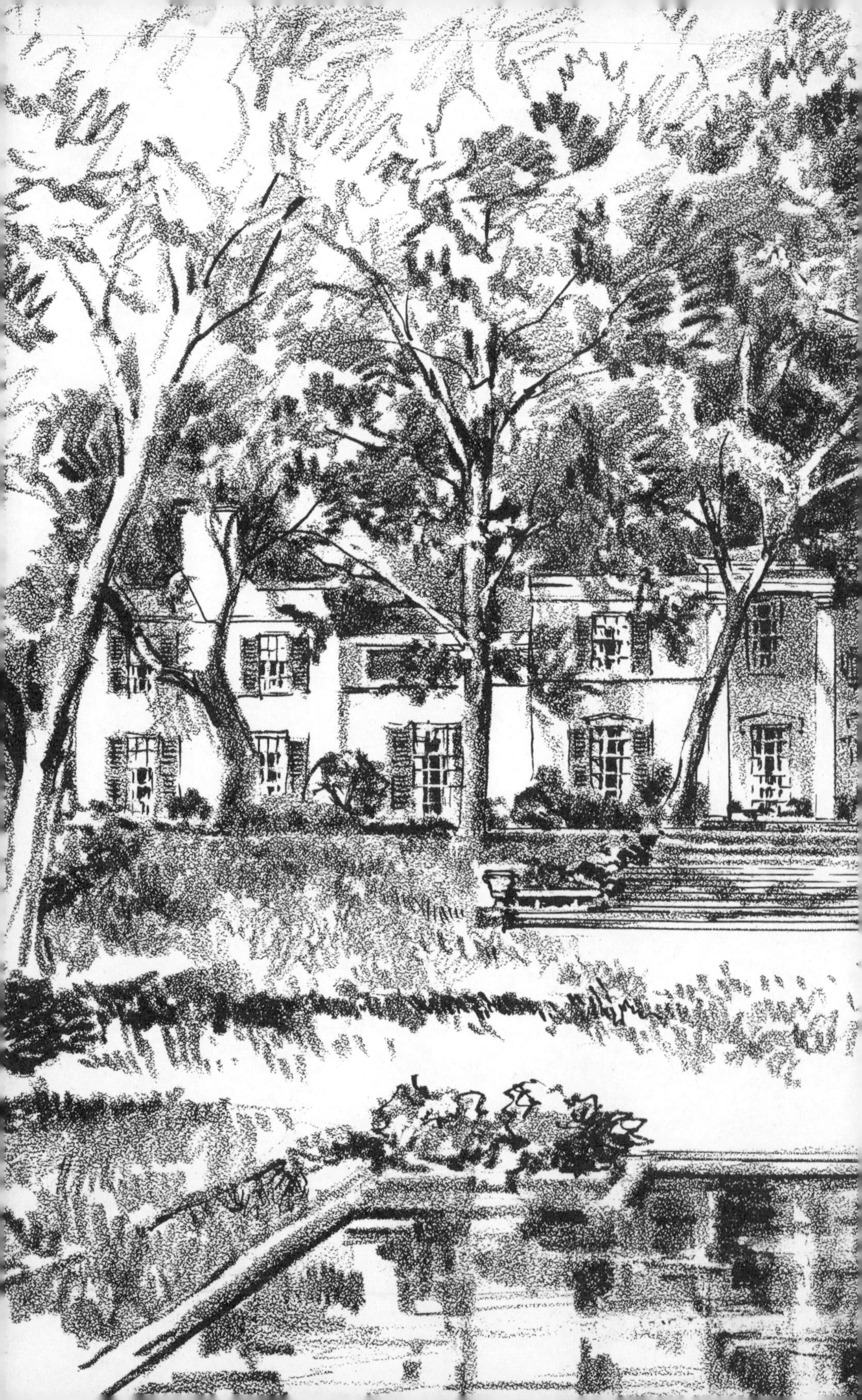